Footpaths

By Debbie Croft

T0342784

Contents

Title	Text Type	Pages
City Footpaths	Information Report	2–9
A Letter to the Council	Exposition	10–16

City Footpaths

A footpath is a path for people to walk along.

Cars and trucks cannot travel on a footpath.

There are footpaths by the sides
of many roads and streets.

People walk on the footpaths
to stay safe from vehicles
that travel on the roads.

There are footpaths on some bridges.

Most bridges have a railing
between the footpath and the road.
The railing stops people
from stepping onto the busy road.

There are footpaths in many parks, too.
People walk around the park on the footpaths.

Sometimes people use these paths
when they are taking their dogs
for a walk.

Some parks have special paths
where people can ride their bikes.

Footpaths help people travel safely
from one place to another.

A Letter to the Council

6 March

Dear Councillors,

I think the council should fix the footpath near our house.

My dad is blind.
Every day he walks to the shops at Hall Street.
He has a long white stick to help him find his way because he does not have a guide dog.

Last week, my dad had an accident
near the corner of Hall Street and Park Road.
He tripped because a tree root
was sticking out of the footpath.

I think the council should dig out the tree root
and put concrete in the hole.

There are other people in the city
who are blind like my dad.

The city council should check
that the footpaths
are safe for everyone.

You must do something to help
because I want my dad to be safe.

Yours sincerely,
Adam Brown